# BEFORE YOU GO...
## TO UNIVERSITY (OR COLLEGE)

THIS WAY UP

BEDDING

Books

PHOTOS

KITCHEN THINGS

DON'T DROP

Your personal, homemade survival guide to leaving home and starting University (or College).

# The idea and story behind
# 'BEFORE YOU GO TO... UNIVERSITY (OR COLLEGE)'
## by Verna Scott-Culkin

**This book idea came about as our daughter was flying the nest and heading off to University.**

**We wanted to give her a 'Personal Survival Guide' to leaving home for the first time and going to University.**

We spent ages trying to find a lovely designed, template type book that family and friends could fill with Love, Wishes, Practical Advice and even Recipes.

We wanted a guide that would fill her heart (and tummy) with joy. But we couldn't find one.

The only University Guides we could find weren't personal or design-based.

They were general rough guides, telling you what to expect, etc. They were written by people who had no idea who our daughter 'was' (like the fact she likes Cheese, but generally only when it's melted over nachos!).

So, we set about creating a brightly designed, templated type book with various headings and subjects to be filled in by loved ones, creating an individual (and also helpful) guide to leaving home and starting University.

Our daughter's book was filled in by lots of family and friends and handed to her as she was getting everything ready to head off on her big adventure.

With other friends children heading off to University this year, we decided to publish this book and we hope they enjoy filling it in as much as we did (beware, it can get quite emotional... but in a good way).

## TO THE FILLER-OUTERS

Mostly this book/journal should be filled in by you with anything you think will help them settle in, whether that's Love, Advice, Recipes or what they could do if they're feeling a little down.

We've also put in a few useful general guides to help your loved one pack and get ready to go.

There's also pages for finance, important addresses, birthdays you may want them to remember and of course a space for an envelope to be stuffed full of wonderful photographs, so they can put them up all around their room.

But mostly this book is about your loved one and let's face it you know them best. Your love, advice and help will get them through that first year.

We hope this book will be practical, helpful and of course individual, but also that it will be a wonderful gift and keepsake for years to come (I still have and use my student cookbook that I hastily copied from my mums recipe book many years ago).

## TO THE HOME LEAVER/UNIVERSITY (COLLEGE) STARTER

We hope you love your book and find it not only helpful but comforting as well. Good Luck on your big adventure, you'll be awesome X.

Before You Go...
to University (or College).
Published by
Verna Scott-Culkin.
Copyright © 2017
Verna Scott-Culkin.

ISBN 978-1-9997023-0-4

Find us on Facebook.

Search 'Before You Go'.

More 'Before...' books
available soon.

email: beforejournals@gmail.com

Book design by Giles Culkin
www.gilesculkin.com

**TO**

...........................................................

**FROM**

...........................................................

**DATE**

...........................................................

THIS WAY UP

BEDDING

Books

PHOTOS

KITCHEN THINGS

DON'T DROP

# WHY WE LOVE YOU

## THERE ARE ALL SORTS OF REASONS...

# WHY WE LOVE YOU

## THERE ARE ALL SORTS OF REASONS...

# WHY WE LOVE YOU

## THERE ARE ALL SORTS OF REASONS...

# WHY WE LOVE YOU

## THERE ARE ALL SORTS OF REASONS...

# WHY WE LOVE YOU

## THERE ARE ALL SORTS OF REASONS...

# IF YOU'RE FEELING BLUE

## *SUGGESTIONS TO PUT A SMILE ON YOUR FACE...

*FILL IN EACH CLOUD WITH THINGS
TO DO THAT YOU
KNOW WILL BRING A SMILE
TO THEIR FACE

# IF YOU'RE FEELING BLUE

## *SUGGESTIONS TO PUT A SMILE ON YOUR FACE...

*FILL IN EACH CLOUD WITH THINGS
TO DO THAT YOU
KNOW WILL BRING A SMILE
TO THEIR FACE

# IF YOU'RE FEELING BLUE

## *SUGGESTIONS TO PUT A SMILE ON YOUR FACE...

*FILL IN EACH CLOUD WITH THINGS
TO DO THAT YOU
KNOW WILL BRING A SMILE
TO THEIR FACE

# ADVICE & TIPS FROM LOVED ONES

## THINGS YOU MAY NEED TO KNOW ON THE WAY

# ADVICE & TIPS FROM LOVED ONES

## THINGS YOU MAY NEED TO KNOW ON THE WAY

## ADVICE & TIPS FROM LOVED ONES

### THINGS YOU MAY NEED TO KNOW ON THE WAY

# ADVICE & TIPS FROM LOVED ONES

## THINGS YOU MAY NEED TO KNOW ON THE WAY

# RECIPES

THIS RECIPE IS KINDLY DONATED BY:

. . . . . . . . . . . . . . . . . . . . . . . . . . . . . . . . . . . . . . . . . . . . . . . .

AND IS CALLED:

. . . . . . . . . . . . . . . . . . . . . . . . . . . . . . . . . . . . . . . . . . . . . . . .

THIS RECIPE SERVES: . . . . . . . .    PREP TIME: . . . . . . . . . .    COOK TIME: . . . . . . . . . . . . . .

| WHAT YOU DO: | WHAT YOU NEED: |
|---|---|
| . . . . . . . . . . . . . . . . . . . . . . . . . . . . . | . . . . . . . . . . . . . . . . . . . . . . . . . . . . . |
| . . . . . . . . . . . . . . . . . . . . . . . . . . . . . | . . . . . . . . . . . . . . . . . . . . . . . . . . . . . |
| . . . . . . . . . . . . . . . . . . . . . . . . . . . . . | . . . . . . . . . . . . . . . . . . . . . . . . . . . . . |
| . . . . . . . . . . . . . . . . . . . . . . . . . . . . . | . . . . . . . . . . . . . . . . . . . . . . . . . . . . . |
| . . . . . . . . . . . . . . . . . . . . . . . . . . . . . | . . . . . . . . . . . . . . . . . . . . . . . . . . . . . |
| . . . . . . . . . . . . . . . . . . . . . . . . . . . . . | . . . . . . . . . . . . . . . . . . . . . . . . . . . . . |
| . . . . . . . . . . . . . . . . . . . . . . . . . . . . . | . . . . . . . . . . . . . . . . . . . . . . . . . . . . . |
| . . . . . . . . . . . . . . . . . . . . . . . . . . . . . | . . . . . . . . . . . . . . . . . . . . . . . . . . . . . |
| . . . . . . . . . . . . . . . . . . . . . . . . . . . . . | . . . . . . . . . . . . . . . . . . . . . . . . . . . . . |
| . . . . . . . . . . . . . . . . . . . . . . . . . . . . . | . . . . . . . . . . . . . . . . . . . . . . . . . . . . . |
| . . . . . . . . . . . . . . . . . . . . . . . . . . . . . | . . . . . . . . . . . . . . . . . . . . . . . . . . . . . |
| . . . . . . . . . . . . . . . . . . . . . . . . . . . . . | . . . . . . . . . . . . . . . . . . . . . . . . . . . . . |
| . . . . . . . . . . . . . . . . . . . . . . . . . . . . . | . . . . . . . . . . . . . . . . . . . . . . . . . . . . . |
| . . . . . . . . . . . . . . . . . . . . . . . . . . . . . | . . . . . . . . . . . . . . . . . . . . . . . . . . . . . |
| . . . . . . . . . . . . . . . . . . . . . . . . . . . . . | . . . . . . . . . . . . . . . . . . . . . . . . . . . . . |
| . . . . . . . . . . . . . . . . . . . . . . . . . . . . . | . . . . . . . . . . . . . . . . . . . . . . . . . . . . . |
| . . . . . . . . . . . . . . . . . . . . . . . . . . . . . | . . . . . . . . . . . . . . . . . . . . . . . . . . . . . |
| . . . . . . . . . . . . . . . . . . . . . . . . . . . . . | . . . . . . . . . . . . . . . . . . . . . . . . . . . . . |
| . . . . . . . . . . . . . . . . . . . . . . . . . . . . . | . . . . . . . . . . . . . . . . . . . . . . . . . . . . . |
| . . . . . . . . . . . . . . . . . . . . . . . . . . . . . | . . . . . . . . . . . . . . . . . . . . . . . . . . . . . |
| . . . . . . . . . . . . . . . . . . . . . . . . . . . . . | . . . . . . . . . . . . . . . . . . . . . . . . . . . . . |

MAKE IT GO FURTHER?        FREEZE?            EAT COLD?            REHEAT?

———————— ★ ★ ————————

THIS RECIPE IS KINDLY DONATED BY:

. . . . . . . . . . . . . . . . . . . . . . . . . . . . . . . . . . . . . . . . . . . . . . . . . . . .

AND IS CALLED:

# RECIPES

. . . . . . . . . . . . . . . . . . . . . . . . . . . . . . . . . . . . . . . . . . . . . . . . . . . .

THIS RECIPE SERVES:. . . . . . . .     PREP TIME:. . . . . . . . . .     COOK TIME:. . . . . . . . . . . . . .

WHAT YOU DO:

WHAT YOU NEED:

MAKE IT GO FURTHER?          FREEZE?               EAT COLD?               REHEAT?

★ ★

# RECIPES

THIS RECIPE IS KINDLY DONATED BY:

. . . . . . . . . . . . . . . . . . . . . . . . . . . . . . . . . . . . . . . . . . . . . . . . . . . . . . . .

AND IS CALLED:

. . . . . . . . . . . . . . . . . . . . . . . . . . . . . . . . . . . . . . . . . . . . . . . . . . . . . . . .

THIS RECIPE SERVES: . . . . . . . .    PREP TIME: . . . . . . . . . .    COOK TIME: . . . . . . . . . . . . . .

| WHAT YOU DO: | WHAT YOU NEED: |
|---|---|
| | |

MAKE IT GO FURTHER?        FREEZE?              EAT COLD?            REHEAT?

★ ★

THIS RECIPE IS KINDLY DONATED BY:

. . . . . . . . . . . . . . . . . . . . . . . . . . . . . . . . . . . . . . . . . . .

AND IS CALLED:

# RECIPES

. . . . . . . . . . . . . . . . . . . . . . . . . . . . . . . . . . . . . . . . . . .

THIS RECIPE SERVES: . . . . . . .    PREP TIME: . . . . . . . . . .    COOK TIME: . . . . . . . . . . . . . .

**WHAT YOU DO:**                                              **WHAT YOU NEED:**

MAKE IT GO FURTHER?        FREEZE?              EAT COLD?              REHEAT?

★ ★

# RECIPES

**THIS RECIPE IS KINDLY DONATED BY:**

. . . . . . . . . . . . . . . . . . . . . . . . . . . . . . . . . . . . . . . . . . . . . . . . . . . . . . . . . . . .

**AND IS CALLED:**

. . . . . . . . . . . . . . . . . . . . . . . . . . . . . . . . . . . . . . . . . . . . . . . . . . . . . . . . . . . .

**THIS RECIPE SERVES:** . . . . . . . . .     **PREP TIME:** . . . . . . . . . .     **COOK TIME:** . . . . . . . . . . . . . .

**WHAT YOU DO:**

**WHAT YOU NEED:**

**MAKE IT GO FURTHER?**     **FREEZE?**     **EAT COLD?**     **REHEAT?**

★ ★

THIS RECIPE IS KINDLY DONATED BY:

. . . . . . . . . . . . . . . . . . . . . . . . . . . . . . . . . . . . . . . . . . . . . . . .

AND IS CALLED:

## RECIPES

. . . . . . . . . . . . . . . . . . . . . . . . . . . . . . . . . . . . . . . . . . . . . . . .

---

THIS RECIPE SERVES: . . . . . . .     PREP TIME: . . . . . . . . . .     COOK TIME: . . . . . . . . . . . . . .

**WHAT YOU DO:**                                                        **WHAT YOU NEED:**

| | |
|---|---|
| . . . . . . . . . . . . . . . . . . . . . . . . . . . | . . . . . . . . . . . . . . . . . . . . . . . . . . . |
| . . . . . . . . . . . . . . . . . . . . . . . . . . . | . . . . . . . . . . . . . . . . . . . . . . . . . . . |
| . . . . . . . . . . . . . . . . . . . . . . . . . . . | . . . . . . . . . . . . . . . . . . . . . . . . . . . |
| . . . . . . . . . . . . . . . . . . . . . . . . . . . | . . . . . . . . . . . . . . . . . . . . . . . . . . . |
| . . . . . . . . . . . . . . . . . . . . . . . . . . . | . . . . . . . . . . . . . . . . . . . . . . . . . . . |
| . . . . . . . . . . . . . . . . . . . . . . . . . . . | . . . . . . . . . . . . . . . . . . . . . . . . . . . |

**MAKE IT GO FURTHER?**     **FREEZE?**     **EAT COLD?**     **REHEAT?**

———————— ★ ★ ————————

## RECIPES

THIS RECIPE IS KINDLY DONATED BY:

. . . . . . . . . . . . . . . . . . . . . . . . . . . . . . . . . . . . . . . . . . . . . . . . . . . . . . . .

AND IS CALLED:

. . . . . . . . . . . . . . . . . . . . . . . . . . . . . . . . . . . . . . . . . . . . . . . . . . . . . . . .

THIS RECIPE SERVES: . . . . . . . .     PREP TIME: . . . . . . . . . .     COOK TIME: . . . . . . . . . . . . . .

| WHAT YOU DO: | WHAT YOU NEED: |
|---|---|
| . . . . . . . . . . . . . . . . . . . . . . . . . . . . . . . . . . . . . . . . | . . . . . . . . . . . . . . . . . . . . . . . . . . . . . . . . . . . . . . . . |
| . . . . . . . . . . . . . . . . . . . . . . . . . . . . . . . . . . . . . . . . | . . . . . . . . . . . . . . . . . . . . . . . . . . . . . . . . . . . . . . . . |
| . . . . . . . . . . . . . . . . . . . . . . . . . . . . . . . . . . . . . . . . | . . . . . . . . . . . . . . . . . . . . . . . . . . . . . . . . . . . . . . . . |
| . . . . . . . . . . . . . . . . . . . . . . . . . . . . . . . . . . . . . . . . | . . . . . . . . . . . . . . . . . . . . . . . . . . . . . . . . . . . . . . . . |
| . . . . . . . . . . . . . . . . . . . . . . . . . . . . . . . . . . . . . . . . | . . . . . . . . . . . . . . . . . . . . . . . . . . . . . . . . . . . . . . . . |
| . . . . . . . . . . . . . . . . . . . . . . . . . . . . . . . . . . . . . . . . | . . . . . . . . . . . . . . . . . . . . . . . . . . . . . . . . . . . . . . . . |
| . . . . . . . . . . . . . . . . . . . . . . . . . . . . . . . . . . . . . . . . | . . . . . . . . . . . . . . . . . . . . . . . . . . . . . . . . . . . . . . . . |
| . . . . . . . . . . . . . . . . . . . . . . . . . . . . . . . . . . . . . . . . | . . . . . . . . . . . . . . . . . . . . . . . . . . . . . . . . . . . . . . . . |

MAKE IT GO FURTHER?     FREEZE?     EAT COLD?     REHEAT?

———————— ★ ★ ————————

RECIPES

THIS RECIPE IS KINDLY DONATED BY:

. . . . . . . . . . . . . . . . . . . . . . . . . . . . . . . . . . . . . . . . . . . . . . . . . . . . .

AND IS CALLED:

. . . . . . . . . . . . . . . . . . . . . . . . . . . . . . . . . . . . . . . . . . . . . . . . . . . . .

THIS RECIPE SERVES: . . . . . . .    PREP TIME: . . . . . . . . . .    COOK TIME: . . . . . . . . . . . . . . .

**WHAT YOU DO:**                          **WHAT YOU NEED:**

MAKE IT GO FURTHER?      FREEZE?           EAT COLD?          REHEAT?

# RECIPES

THIS RECIPE IS KINDLY DONATED BY:

. . . . . . . . . . . . . . . . . . . . . . . . . . . . . . . . . . . . . . . . . . . . .

AND IS CALLED:

. . . . . . . . . . . . . . . . . . . . . . . . . . . . . . . . . . . . . . . . . . . . .

THIS RECIPE SERVES: . . . . . . . .     PREP TIME: . . . . . . . . . .     COOK TIME: . . . . . . . . . . . . . . .

| WHAT YOU DO: | WHAT YOU NEED: |
|---|---|
| . . . . . . . . . . . . . . . . . . . . . . . . | . . . . . . . . . . . . . . . . . . . . . . . . |
| . . . . . . . . . . . . . . . . . . . . . . . . | . . . . . . . . . . . . . . . . . . . . . . . . |
| . . . . . . . . . . . . . . . . . . . . . . . . | . . . . . . . . . . . . . . . . . . . . . . . . |
| . . . . . . . . . . . . . . . . . . . . . . . . | . . . . . . . . . . . . . . . . . . . . . . . . |
| . . . . . . . . . . . . . . . . . . . . . . . . | . . . . . . . . . . . . . . . . . . . . . . . . |
| . . . . . . . . . . . . . . . . . . . . . . . . | . . . . . . . . . . . . . . . . . . . . . . . . |
| . . . . . . . . . . . . . . . . . . . . . . . . | . . . . . . . . . . . . . . . . . . . . . . . . |
| . . . . . . . . . . . . . . . . . . . . . . . . | . . . . . . . . . . . . . . . . . . . . . . . . |
| . . . . . . . . . . . . . . . . . . . . . . . . | . . . . . . . . . . . . . . . . . . . . . . . . |
| . . . . . . . . . . . . . . . . . . . . . . . . | . . . . . . . . . . . . . . . . . . . . . . . . |
| . . . . . . . . . . . . . . . . . . . . . . . . | . . . . . . . . . . . . . . . . . . . . . . . . |
| . . . . . . . . . . . . . . . . . . . . . . . . | . . . . . . . . . . . . . . . . . . . . . . . . |
| . . . . . . . . . . . . . . . . . . . . . . . . | . . . . . . . . . . . . . . . . . . . . . . . . |
| . . . . . . . . . . . . . . . . . . . . . . . . | . . . . . . . . . . . . . . . . . . . . . . . . |
| . . . . . . . . . . . . . . . . . . . . . . . . | . . . . . . . . . . . . . . . . . . . . . . . . |
| . . . . . . . . . . . . . . . . . . . . . . . . | . . . . . . . . . . . . . . . . . . . . . . . . |
| . . . . . . . . . . . . . . . . . . . . . . . . | . . . . . . . . . . . . . . . . . . . . . . . . |
| . . . . . . . . . . . . . . . . . . . . . . . . | . . . . . . . . . . . . . . . . . . . . . . . . |

MAKE IT GO FURTHER?     FREEZE?     EAT COLD?     REHEAT?

★ ★

THIS RECIPE IS KINDLY DONATED BY:

. . . . . . . . . . . . . . . . . . . . . . . . . . . . . . . . . . . . . . . . . . . . . . .

AND IS CALLED:

# RECIPES

. . . . . . . . . . . . . . . . . . . . . . . . . . . . . . . . . . . . . . . . . . . . . . .

THIS RECIPE SERVES:. . . . . . . .     PREP TIME: . . . . . . . . . .     COOK TIME: . . . . . . . . . . . . . .

**WHAT YOU DO:**

**WHAT YOU NEED:**

. . . . . . . . . . . . . . . . . . . . . . . . . . . . . . . . . . . . . . . . . . . . . . .
. . . . . . . . . . . . . . . . . . . . . . . . . . . . . . . . . . . . . . . . . . . . . . .
. . . . . . . . . . . . . . . . . . . . . . . . . . . . . . . . . . . . . . . . . . . . . . .
. . . . . . . . . . . . . . . . . . . . . . . . . . . . . . . . . . . . . . . . . . . . . . .
. . . . . . . . . . . . . . . . . . . . . . . . . . . . . . . . . . . . . . . . . . . . . . .
. . . . . . . . . . . . . . . . . . . . . . . . . . . . . . . . . . . . . . . . . . . . . . .
. . . . . . . . . . . . . . . . . . . . . . . . . . . . . . . . . . . . . . . . . . . . . . .
. . . . . . . . . . . . . . . . . . . . . . . . . . . . . . . . . . . . . . . . . . . . . . .
. . . . . . . . . . . . . . . . . . . . . . . . . . . . . . . . . . . . . . . . . . . . . . .
. . . . . . . . . . . . . . . . . . . . . . . . . . . . . . . . . . . . . . . . . . . . . . .
. . . . . . . . . . . . . . . . . . . . . . . . . . . . . . . . . . . . . . . . . . . . . . .
. . . . . . . . . . . . . . . . . . . . . . . . . . . . . . . . . . . . . . . . . . . . . . .
. . . . . . . . . . . . . . . . . . . . . . . . . . . . . . . . . . . . . . . . . . . . . . .
. . . . . . . . . . . . . . . . . . . . . . . . . . . . . . . . . . . . . . . . . . . . . . .
. . . . . . . . . . . . . . . . . . . . . . . . . . . . . . . . . . . . . . . . . . . . . . .
. . . . . . . . . . . . . . . . . . . . . . . . . . . . . . . . . . . . . . . . . . . . . . .
. . . . . . . . . . . . . . . . . . . . . . . . . . . . . . . . . . . . . . . . . . . . . . .
. . . . . . . . . . . . . . . . . . . . . . . . . . . . . . . . . . . . . . . . . . . . . . .
. . . . . . . . . . . . . . . . . . . . . . . . . . . . . . . . . . . . . . . . . . . . . . .
. . . . . . . . . . . . . . . . . . . . . . . . . . . . . . . . . . . . . . . . . . . . . . .

**MAKE IT GO FURTHER?**     **FREEZE?**     **EAT COLD?**     **REHEAT?**

★ ★

# RECIPES

THIS RECIPE IS KINDLY DONATED BY:

. . . . . . . . . . . . . . . . . . . . . . . . . . . . . . . . . . . . . . . . . . . . .

AND IS CALLED:

. . . . . . . . . . . . . . . . . . . . . . . . . . . . . . . . . . . . . . . . . . . . .

THIS RECIPE SERVES: . . . . . . . .     PREP TIME: . . . . . . . . . .     COOK TIME: . . . . . . . . . . . . . .

WHAT YOU DO: | WHAT YOU NEED:
--- | ---

MAKE IT GO FURTHER?          FREEZE?          EAT COLD?          REHEAT?

THIS RECIPE IS KINDLY DONATED BY:

. . . . . . . . . . . . . . . . . . . . . . . . . . . . . . . . . . . . . . . . . . . . . . . . . . . . . .

AND IS CALLED:

RECIPES

. . . . . . . . . . . . . . . . . . . . . . . . . . . . . . . . . . . . . . . . . . . . . . . . . . . . . .

THIS RECIPE SERVES:. . . . . . . .    PREP TIME: . . . . . . . . . .    COOK TIME: . . . . . . . . . .

WHAT YOU DO:                                              WHAT YOU NEED:

| WHAT YOU DO: | WHAT YOU NEED: |
|---|---|

MAKE IT GO FURTHER?        FREEZE?            EAT COLD?            REHEAT?

★ ★

THIS RECIPE IS KINDLY DONATED BY:

. . . . . . . . . . . . . . . . . . . . . . . . . . . . . . . . . . . . . . . . . . . . . . . . .

AND IS CALLED:

## RECIPES

. . . . . . . . . . . . . . . . . . . . . . . . . . . . . . . . . . . . . . . . . . . . . . . . .

THIS RECIPE SERVES: . . . . . . . .    PREP TIME: . . . . . . . . . .    COOK TIME: . . . . . . . . . . . . . .

**WHAT YOU DO:**                                          **WHAT YOU NEED:**

. . . . . . . . . . . . . . . . . . . . . . . . . .    . . . . . . . . . . . . . . . . . . . . . .

. . . . . . . . . . . . . . . . . . . . . . . . . .    . . . . . . . . . . . . . . . . . . . . . .

. . . . . . . . . . . . . . . . . . . . . . . . . .    . . . . . . . . . . . . . . . . . . . . . .

. . . . . . . . . . . . . . . . . . . . . . . . . .    . . . . . . . . . . . . . . . . . . . . . .

. . . . . . . . . . . . . . . . . . . . . . . . . .    . . . . . . . . . . . . . . . . . . . . . .

. . . . . . . . . . . . . . . . . . . . . . . . . .    . . . . . . . . . . . . . . . . . . . . . .

. . . . . . . . . . . . . . . . . . . . . . . . . .    . . . . . . . . . . . . . . . . . . . . . .

. . . . . . . . . . . . . . . . . . . . . . . . . .    . . . . . . . . . . . . . . . . . . . . . .

. . . . . . . . . . . . . . . . . . . . . . . . . .    . . . . . . . . . . . . . . . . . . . . . .

. . . . . . . . . . . . . . . . . . . . . . . . . .    . . . . . . . . . . . . . . . . . . . . . .

. . . . . . . . . . . . . . . . . . . . . . . . . .    . . . . . . . . . . . . . . . . . . . . . .

. . . . . . . . . . . . . . . . . . . . . . . . . .    . . . . . . . . . . . . . . . . . . . . . .

. . . . . . . . . . . . . . . . . . . . . . . . . .    . . . . . . . . . . . . . . . . . . . . . .

. . . . . . . . . . . . . . . . . . . . . . . . . .    . . . . . . . . . . . . . . . . . . . . . .

. . . . . . . . . . . . . . . . . . . . . . . . . .    . . . . . . . . . . . . . . . . . . . . . .

. . . . . . . . . . . . . . . . . . . . . . . . . .    . . . . . . . . . . . . . . . . . . . . . .

. . . . . . . . . . . . . . . . . . . . . . . . . .    . . . . . . . . . . . . . . . . . . . . . .

. . . . . . . . . . . . . . . . . . . . . . . . . .    . . . . . . . . . . . . . . . . . . . . . .

. . . . . . . . . . . . . . . . . . . . . . . . . .    . . . . . . . . . . . . . . . . . . . . . .

. . . . . . . . . . . . . . . . . . . . . . . . . .    . . . . . . . . . . . . . . . . . . . . . .

. . . . . . . . . . . . . . . . . . . . . . . . . .    . . . . . . . . . . . . . . . . . . . . . .

. . . . . . . . . . . . . . . . . . . . . . . . . .    . . . . . . . . . . . . . . . . . . . . . .

. . . . . . . . . . . . . . . . . . . . . . . . . .    . . . . . . . . . . . . . . . . . . . . . .

MAKE IT GO FURTHER?        FREEZE?              EAT COLD?              REHEAT?

———————— ★ ★ ————————

RECIPES

THIS RECIPE IS KINDLY DONATED BY:

. . . . . . . . . . . . . . . . . . . . . . . . . . . . . . . . . . . . . . . . . . . . . . . . .

AND IS CALLED:

. . . . . . . . . . . . . . . . . . . . . . . . . . . . . . . . . . . . . . . . . . . . . . . . .

THIS RECIPE SERVES:. . . . . . . .     PREP TIME: . . . . . . . . . .     COOK TIME: . . . . . . . . . . . . . .

**WHAT YOU DO:**

| **WHAT YOU NEED:** |

MAKE IT GO FURTHER?          FREEZE?                    EAT COLD?                    REHEAT?

★ ★

## RECIPES

THIS RECIPE IS KINDLY DONATED BY:

. . . . . . . . . . . . . . . . . . . . . . . . . . . . . . . . . . . . . . . . . . . . . . . . . .

AND IS CALLED:

. . . . . . . . . . . . . . . . . . . . . . . . . . . . . . . . . . . . . . . . . . . . . . . . . .

THIS RECIPE SERVES: . . . . . . . .     PREP TIME: . . . . . . . . . .     COOK TIME: . . . . . . . . . . . . . .

**WHAT YOU DO:**                                              **WHAT YOU NEED:**

MAKE IT GO FURTHER?        FREEZE?              EAT COLD?              REHEAT?

★ ★

# RECIPES

THIS RECIPE IS KINDLY DONATED BY:

. . . . . . . . . . . . . . . . . . . . . . . . . . . . . . . . . . . . . . . . . . . . .

AND IS CALLED:

. . . . . . . . . . . . . . . . . . . . . . . . . . . . . . . . . . . . . . . . . . . . .

THIS RECIPE SERVES: . . . . . . .     PREP TIME: . . . . . . . . . .     COOK TIME: . . . . . . . . . . . . . .

| WHAT YOU DO: | WHAT YOU NEED: |
|---|---|
| | |

MAKE IT GO FURTHER?          FREEZE?          EAT COLD?          REHEAT?

★ ★

# RECIPES

THIS RECIPE IS KINDLY DONATED BY:

. . . . . . . . . . . . . . . . . . . . . . . . . . . . . . . . . . . . . . . . . . . .

AND IS CALLED:

. . . . . . . . . . . . . . . . . . . . . . . . . . . . . . . . . . . . . . . . . . . .

THIS RECIPE SERVES: . . . . . . . .     PREP TIME: . . . . . . . . .     COOK TIME: . . . . . . . . . . . . .

**WHAT YOU DO:**

. . . . . . . . . . . . . . . . . . . . . . . . . . . . . . . . . . . . . . . . . . .
. . . . . . . . . . . . . . . . . . . . . . . . . . . . . . . . . . . . . . . . . . .
. . . . . . . . . . . . . . . . . . . . . . . . . . . . . . . . . . . . . . . . . . .
. . . . . . . . . . . . . . . . . . . . . . . . . . . . . . . . . . . . . . . . . . .
. . . . . . . . . . . . . . . . . . . . . . . . . . . . . . . . . . . . . . . . . . .
. . . . . . . . . . . . . . . . . . . . . . . . . . . . . . . . . . . . . . . . . . .
. . . . . . . . . . . . . . . . . . . . . . . . . . . . . . . . . . . . . . . . . . .
. . . . . . . . . . . . . . . . . . . . . . . . . . . . . . . . . . . . . . . . . . .
. . . . . . . . . . . . . . . . . . . . . . . . . . . . . . . . . . . . . . . . . . .
. . . . . . . . . . . . . . . . . . . . . . . . . . . . . . . . . . . . . . . . . . .
. . . . . . . . . . . . . . . . . . . . . . . . . . . . . . . . . . . . . . . . . . .
. . . . . . . . . . . . . . . . . . . . . . . . . . . . . . . . . . . . . . . . . . .
. . . . . . . . . . . . . . . . . . . . . . . . . . . . . . . . . . . . . . . . . . .
. . . . . . . . . . . . . . . . . . . . . . . . . . . . . . . . . . . . . . . . . . .
. . . . . . . . . . . . . . . . . . . . . . . . . . . . . . . . . . . . . . . . . . .
. . . . . . . . . . . . . . . . . . . . . . . . . . . . . . . . . . . . . . . . . . .
. . . . . . . . . . . . . . . . . . . . . . . . . . . . . . . . . . . . . . . . . . .
. . . . . . . . . . . . . . . . . . . . . . . . . . . . . . . . . . . . . . . . . . .
. . . . . . . . . . . . . . . . . . . . . . . . . . . . . . . . . . . . . . . . . . .
. . . . . . . . . . . . . . . . . . . . . . . . . . . . . . . . . . . . . . . . . . .
. . . . . . . . . . . . . . . . . . . . . . . . . . . . . . . . . . . . . . . . . . .

**WHAT YOU NEED:**

. . . . . . . . . . . . . . . . . . . . . . . . . . . . . . . . . .
. . . . . . . . . . . . . . . . . . . . . . . . . . . . . . . . . .
. . . . . . . . . . . . . . . . . . . . . . . . . . . . . . . . . .
. . . . . . . . . . . . . . . . . . . . . . . . . . . . . . . . . .
. . . . . . . . . . . . . . . . . . . . . . . . . . . . . . . . . .
. . . . . . . . . . . . . . . . . . . . . . . . . . . . . . . . . .
. . . . . . . . . . . . . . . . . . . . . . . . . . . . . . . . . .
. . . . . . . . . . . . . . . . . . . . . . . . . . . . . . . . . .
. . . . . . . . . . . . . . . . . . . . . . . . . . . . . . . . . .
. . . . . . . . . . . . . . . . . . . . . . . . . . . . . . . . . .
. . . . . . . . . . . . . . . . . . . . . . . . . . . . . . . . . .
. . . . . . . . . . . . . . . . . . . . . . . . . . . . . . . . . .
. . . . . . . . . . . . . . . . . . . . . . . . . . . . . . . . . .
. . . . . . . . . . . . . . . . . . . . . . . . . . . . . . . . . .
. . . . . . . . . . . . . . . . . . . . . . . . . . . . . . . . . .
. . . . . . . . . . . . . . . . . . . . . . . . . . . . . . . . . .
. . . . . . . . . . . . . . . . . . . . . . . . . . . . . . . . . .
. . . . . . . . . . . . . . . . . . . . . . . . . . . . . . . . . .
. . . . . . . . . . . . . . . . . . . . . . . . . . . . . . . . . .
. . . . . . . . . . . . . . . . . . . . . . . . . . . . . . . . . .
. . . . . . . . . . . . . . . . . . . . . . . . . . . . . . . . . .

MAKE IT GO FURTHER?     FREEZE?     EAT COLD?     REHEAT?

★ ★

RECIPES

THiS RECiPE iS KiNDLY DONATED BY:

. . . . . . . . . . . . . . . . . . . . . . . . . . . . . . . . . . . . . . . . . . . . . . . . . . . . .

AND iS CALLED:

. . . . . . . . . . . . . . . . . . . . . . . . . . . . . . . . . . . . . . . . . . . . . . . . . . . . .

THiS RECiPE SERVES:. . . . . . . . .    PREP TiME: . . . . . . . . . .    COOK TiME: . . . . . . . . . . . . . . .

**WHAT YOU DO:**

| **WHAT YOU NEED:** |

MAKE iT GO FURTHER?     FREEZE?          EAT COLD?          REHEAT?

★ ★

# PRACTICAL GUIDES

# Things you may need.

Just a few general lists to...

a) Use

b) Ignore

After all they are just a guide to help you on your way

———— ●●● ————

# PRACTICAL GUIDES

## YOUR ROOM

**Duvet and Pillows** (check the size of your 'new' bed before buying anything)

**Quilt covers**

**Bottom sheets and pillowcases x2 –**

...because, yes you are going to have to change them and WASH them.

**A throw for the bed –**

...keeps your quilt cleaner, and you warmer.

**Mattress protector**

**Hot Water bottle**

**Earplugs**

**Bath and Hand towels**

**Flannel**

**Favourite Photos –** lots of them

**Clock/Radio/alarm –**

...because you don't want to miss those lovely early morning lectures.

**Door wedge –** so you can see and hear people coming and going.
(Unless it's a fire door)

**Box of chocolates or bottle of bubbly –** celebrate arriving and
everyone makes friends more quickly when chocolate or drink is involved.

**Board Game/Pack of Cards**

**Anything else...**

## Anything else...

## CLOTHES

Everyday – jeans, tops, jumpers, t-shirts etc.

Remember it might be warm at the start of term, it may not be like that by the end

UNDERWEAR!

PJs and dressing gown

Coats, hats, scarves, gloves and cosy things.

Shoes, boots, trainers, heels

Night Out clothes – an important section of your wardrobe, obviously

Work or Interview clothes

Fitness/Gym stuff

Over door hooks

Coat hangers

Fancy Dress items

Weekend bag for travelling home

## WASHING – because you are going to have to wash most of the above!

Washing Powder/Tablets/2-in-one liquid with conditioner – makes everything smell nice

Basket for all the dirty stuff

Mini airer/clothes horse – as there are only so many doors and chairs you can drape stuff on

Iron, if you like Ironing

## WASHING SYMBOLS

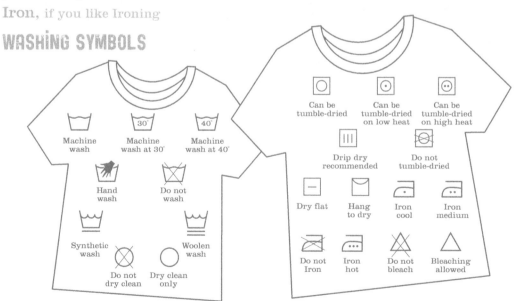

Separate dark and light clothes (however tempting it is to put them all in together).

Check all pockets before washing (tissues, headphones, hair grips, money – it's amazing what you can find!)

Anything else…

# PRACTICAL GUIDES

## PERSONAL STUFF

Shampoo/Conditioner – Hair Stuff

Shower Gel / Soap

Facial stuff - Make Up

Smellies

Razors

Toothpaste/Toothbrush

Personal items

Anything else...

Anything else...

# PRACTICAL GUIDES

## MEDICINE CHEST

Register with the local doctor/dentsist
Think about getting up-to-date with any injections before you go
Painkillers
Plasters
Cold/Flu Remedy
Hangover Remedy
Antiseptic cream
Scissors
Vitamins
Tweezers

Anything else...

## Anything else...

# PRACTICAL GUIDES

## FOOD AND KiTCHEN STUFF

Whether it's supplied (lucky you) or not, you may want some of these things if you want to eat...

Kettle
Toaster
Saucepans – 1 big/1 small
Oven proof dish with lid
Frying pan
Baking trays
Scissors
Grater
Peeler/Masher
Tin Opener
Sieve
Whisk
Plastic containers – to store leftovers or put sandwiches in
Cling Film
Foil (DON'T PUT FOIL IN MICROWAVE – it's not big or clever!)
Knives
Bottle Opener, Cork Screw
Plates, Bowls, Cutlery, Mugs, Glasses

Washing Up Stuff - liquid, cloths, bin bags, anti bacterial spray
Tea Towels – at least 4 (keep one hidden in your room) as these will get used for every spill, accident and no doubt even after washing they'll look like they could stand up on their own!

Anything else...

## FOOD

From staples to luxuries, the favourite foods you're used to at home can make leaving a little easier (see recipe pages), on these next few pages we've given you room to create your own regular shopping lists that you can work from.

**Staples – every day things Milk, Bread...**

# PRACTICAL GUIDES

## FOOD

From staples to luxuries, the favourite foods you're used to at home can make leaving a little easier (see recipe pages), on these next few pages we've given you room to create your own regular shopping lists that you can work from.

### Weekly – Rice, Pasta...

## FOOD

From staples to luxuries, the favourite foods you're used to at home can make leaving a little easier (see recipe pages), on these next few pages we've given you room to create your own regular shopping lists that you can work from.

### Monthly – Tins, etc.

# PRACTICAL GUIDES

## FOOD

From staples to luxuries, the favourite foods you're used to at home can make leaving a little easier (see recipe pages), on these next few pages we've given you room to create your own regular shopping lists that you can work from.

### Freezer stuff

# FOOD

From staples to luxuries, the favourite foods you're used to at home can make leaving a little easier (see recipe pages), on these next few pages we've given you room to create your own regular shopping lists that you can work from.

## Non Food Items – Toothpaste, Bin Bags, etc.

# PRACTICAL GUIDES

## CLEANING

Antibacterial Wipes – a gift from the angels! Cleans allsorts
Bathroom Cleaner
Bleach
Toilet Cleaner and Brush
Air Freshener
Floor Cloth

Anything else...

## Anything else…

# PRACTICAL GUIDES

## NOT FORGETTING WHY YOU ARE THERE.
## STUDY STUFF

This Book!
Notice/Pin board and pins (of course)
Note books/A4 paper/Post It Notes
Refill Pads and plastic sleeves
A4 Binders
A4 display book, for slipping things in.
Pens/Pencils/Highlighters/Ruler/Eraser/Sharpener
Scissors
Hole Punch
Sticky tape/Blu Tac/Stapler/PaperClips
Calculator
Calendar
Address Book (see this book)
Passport Photos – get some done before you go and get them scanned in so you can always access them for IDs etc. Keep some on the computer at home as well
Take a note of your National Insurance number* (or a copy/scan)
Take a note of your Health Card number* (or a copy/scan)
A photocopy of your Passport*
if you do not want the responsibility of having it with you at University.
Exam Certificates* (if required)
Letters and documents regarding University & Accommodation*
Student Finance/Loan documents*
Banking Stuff - Cheque book. Paying in book
Debit/Credit card
Insurance documents for anything valuable*
Travel Cards – Train. Bus etc.
Driving Licence*
CV

*Make sure you keep any copies of important documents at home just in case anything goes missing.

— ••• —

Anything else...

# PRACTICAL GUIDES

## OTHER THINGS –

Phone
Laptop
iPod/iPad
Speakers
Chargers for everything – and we mean everything,
no point them being at home.
Extension leads
Memory Sticks
Battery Fairy Lights
Batteries
TV – check if you'll need a TV license
Radio

Anything else...

# Anything else...

# LOCAL AREA

## SHOPS, BARS, CLUBS, SOCIETIES, ETC.

## TRAINS, BUSES, TAXIS, ETC.

# EMERGENCY NUMBERS

## IMPORTANT TO REMEMBER

DOCTORS: .....................................................................

DENTIST: .....................................................................

ACCOMMODATION/LANDLORD: .....................................................................

UNIVERSITY/COLLEGE: .....................................................................

BANK: .....................................................................

NEIGHBOURS: .....................................................................

ANY OTHERS

## SERIAL NUMBERS
### ANYTHING IMPORTANT THAT COULD GO MISSING? BIKES, LAPTOPS, ETC.

# CONTACTS

NAME: ...........................................................................

ADDRESS: .......................................................................

.......................................................................

.......................................................................

PHONE: ..........................................................................

EMAIL: ..........................................................................

NAME: ...........................................................................

ADDRESS: .......................................................................

.......................................................................

.......................................................................

PHONE: ..........................................................................

EMAIL: ..........................................................................

NAME: ...........................................................................

ADDRESS: .......................................................................

.......................................................................

.......................................................................

PHONE: ..........................................................................

EMAIL: ..........................................................................

NAME: ...........................................................................

ADDRESS: .......................................................................

.......................................................................

.......................................................................

PHONE: ..........................................................................

EMAIL: ..........................................................................

NAME: ...........................................................................

ADDRESS: .......................................................................

.......................................................................

.......................................................................

PHONE: ..........................................................................

EMAIL: ..........................................................................

NAME: .....................................................................
ADDRESS: .................................................................
.....................................................................
PHONE: ...................................................................
EMAIL: ....................................................................

NAME: .....................................................................
ADDRESS: .................................................................
.....................................................................
PHONE: ...................................................................
EMAIL: ....................................................................

NAME: .....................................................................
ADDRESS: .................................................................
.....................................................................
PHONE: ...................................................................
EMAIL: ....................................................................

NAME: .....................................................................
ADDRESS: .................................................................
.....................................................................
PHONE: ...................................................................
EMAIL: ....................................................................

NAME: .....................................................................
ADDRESS: .................................................................
.....................................................................
PHONE: ...................................................................
EMAIL: ....................................................................

## CONTACTS

NAME: ...........................................................................
ADDRESS: .......................................................................
...........................................................................
PHONE: ........................................................................
EMAIL: .........................................................................

NAME: ...........................................................................
ADDRESS: .......................................................................
...........................................................................
PHONE: ........................................................................
EMAIL: .........................................................................

NAME: ...........................................................................
ADDRESS: .......................................................................
...........................................................................
PHONE: ........................................................................
EMAIL: .........................................................................

NAME: ...........................................................................
ADDRESS: .......................................................................
...........................................................................
PHONE: ........................................................................
EMAIL: .........................................................................

NAME: ...........................................................................
ADDRESS: .......................................................................
...........................................................................
PHONE: ........................................................................
EMAIL: .........................................................................

NAME: . . . . . . . . . . . . . . . . . . . . . . . . . . . . . . . . . . . . . . . . . . . . . . . . . . . . . . . . . . . . . . . . . . . . . . . . . . . . . . . . . . . . . . . . . .
ADDRESS: . . . . . . . . . . . . . . . . . . . . . . . . . . . . . . . . . . . . . . . . . . . . . . . . . . . . . . . . . . . . . . . . . . . . . . . . . . . . . . . . . . . . . .

. . . . . . . . . . . . . . . . . . . . . . . . . . . . . . . . . . . . . . . . . . . . . . . . . . . . . . . . . . . . . . . . . . . . . . . . . . . . . . . . . . . . . . . . . . . .

PHONE: . . . . . . . . . . . . . . . . . . . . . . . . . . . . . . . . . . . . . . . . . . . . . . . . . . . . . . . . . . . . . . . . . . . . . . . . . . . . . . . . . . . . . . . .
EMAIL: . . . . . . . . . . . . . . . . . . . . . . . . . . . . . . . . . . . . . . . . . . . . . . . . . . . . . . . . . . . . . . . . . . . . . . . . . . . . . . . . . . . . . . . .

NAME: . . . . . . . . . . . . . . . . . . . . . . . . . . . . . . . . . . . . . . . . . . . . . . . . . . . . . . . . . . . . . . . . . . . . . . . . . . . . . . . . . . . . . . . . . .
ADDRESS: . . . . . . . . . . . . . . . . . . . . . . . . . . . . . . . . . . . . . . . . . . . . . . . . . . . . . . . . . . . . . . . . . . . . . . . . . . . . . . . . . . . . . .

. . . . . . . . . . . . . . . . . . . . . . . . . . . . . . . . . . . . . . . . . . . . . . . . . . . . . . . . . . . . . . . . . . . . . . . . . . . . . . . . . . . . . . . . . . . .

PHONE: . . . . . . . . . . . . . . . . . . . . . . . . . . . . . . . . . . . . . . . . . . . . . . . . . . . . . . . . . . . . . . . . . . . . . . . . . . . . . . . . . . . . . . . .
EMAIL: . . . . . . . . . . . . . . . . . . . . . . . . . . . . . . . . . . . . . . . . . . . . . . . . . . . . . . . . . . . . . . . . . . . . . . . . . . . . . . . . . . . . . . . .

NAME: . . . . . . . . . . . . . . . . . . . . . . . . . . . . . . . . . . . . . . . . . . . . . . . . . . . . . . . . . . . . . . . . . . . . . . . . . . . . . . . . . . . . . . . . . .
ADDRESS: . . . . . . . . . . . . . . . . . . . . . . . . . . . . . . . . . . . . . . . . . . . . . . . . . . . . . . . . . . . . . . . . . . . . . . . . . . . . . . . . . . . . . .

. . . . . . . . . . . . . . . . . . . . . . . . . . . . . . . . . . . . . . . . . . . . . . . . . . . . . . . . . . . . . . . . . . . . . . . . . . . . . . . . . . . . . . . . . . . .

PHONE: . . . . . . . . . . . . . . . . . . . . . . . . . . . . . . . . . . . . . . . . . . . . . . . . . . . . . . . . . . . . . . . . . . . . . . . . . . . . . . . . . . . . . . . .
EMAIL: . . . . . . . . . . . . . . . . . . . . . . . . . . . . . . . . . . . . . . . . . . . . . . . . . . . . . . . . . . . . . . . . . . . . . . . . . . . . . . . . . . . . . . . .

NAME: . . . . . . . . . . . . . . . . . . . . . . . . . . . . . . . . . . . . . . . . . . . . . . . . . . . . . . . . . . . . . . . . . . . . . . . . . . . . . . . . . . . . . . . . . .
ADDRESS: . . . . . . . . . . . . . . . . . . . . . . . . . . . . . . . . . . . . . . . . . . . . . . . . . . . . . . . . . . . . . . . . . . . . . . . . . . . . . . . . . . . . . .

. . . . . . . . . . . . . . . . . . . . . . . . . . . . . . . . . . . . . . . . . . . . . . . . . . . . . . . . . . . . . . . . . . . . . . . . . . . . . . . . . . . . . . . . . . . .

PHONE: . . . . . . . . . . . . . . . . . . . . . . . . . . . . . . . . . . . . . . . . . . . . . . . . . . . . . . . . . . . . . . . . . . . . . . . . . . . . . . . . . . . . . . . .
EMAIL: . . . . . . . . . . . . . . . . . . . . . . . . . . . . . . . . . . . . . . . . . . . . . . . . . . . . . . . . . . . . . . . . . . . . . . . . . . . . . . . . . . . . . . . .

NAME: . . . . . . . . . . . . . . . . . . . . . . . . . . . . . . . . . . . . . . . . . . . . . . . . . . . . . . . . . . . . . . . . . . . . . . . . . . . . . . . . . . . . . . . . . .
ADDRESS: . . . . . . . . . . . . . . . . . . . . . . . . . . . . . . . . . . . . . . . . . . . . . . . . . . . . . . . . . . . . . . . . . . . . . . . . . . . . . . . . . . . . . .

. . . . . . . . . . . . . . . . . . . . . . . . . . . . . . . . . . . . . . . . . . . . . . . . . . . . . . . . . . . . . . . . . . . . . . . . . . . . . . . . . . . . . . . . . . . .

PHONE: . . . . . . . . . . . . . . . . . . . . . . . . . . . . . . . . . . . . . . . . . . . . . . . . . . . . . . . . . . . . . . . . . . . . . . . . . . . . . . . . . . . . . . . .
EMAIL: . . . . . . . . . . . . . . . . . . . . . . . . . . . . . . . . . . . . . . . . . . . . . . . . . . . . . . . . . . . . . . . . . . . . . . . . . . . . . . . . . . . . . . . .

# CONTACTS

NAME: .................................................................................

ADDRESS: ............................................................................

....................................................................................

PHONE: ...............................................................................

EMAIL: ...............................................................................

NAME: .................................................................................

ADDRESS: ............................................................................

....................................................................................

PHONE: ...............................................................................

EMAIL: ...............................................................................

NAME: .................................................................................

ADDRESS: ............................................................................

....................................................................................

PHONE: ...............................................................................

EMAIL: ...............................................................................

NAME: .................................................................................

ADDRESS: ............................................................................

....................................................................................

PHONE: ...............................................................................

EMAIL: ...............................................................................

NAME: .................................................................................

ADDRESS: ............................................................................

....................................................................................

PHONE: ...............................................................................

EMAIL: ...............................................................................

**NAME:** ......................................................................................................................
**ADDRESS:** ................................................................................................................
............................................................................................................................
**PHONE:** ....................................................................................................................
**EMAIL:** ....................................................................................................................

**NAME:** ......................................................................................................................
**ADDRESS:** ................................................................................................................
............................................................................................................................
**PHONE:** ....................................................................................................................
**EMAIL:** ....................................................................................................................

**NAME:** ......................................................................................................................
**ADDRESS:** ................................................................................................................
............................................................................................................................
**PHONE:** ....................................................................................................................
**EMAIL:** ....................................................................................................................

**NAME:** ......................................................................................................................
**ADDRESS:** ................................................................................................................
............................................................................................................................
**PHONE:** ....................................................................................................................
**EMAIL:** ....................................................................................................................

**NAME:** ......................................................................................................................
**ADDRESS:** ................................................................................................................
............................................................................................................................
**PHONE:** ....................................................................................................................
**EMAIL:** ....................................................................................................................

# CONTACTS

NAME: ............................................................................

ADDRESS: ........................................................................

............................................................................

............................................................................

PHONE: ..........................................................................

EMAIL: ..........................................................................

NAME: ............................................................................

ADDRESS: ........................................................................

............................................................................

............................................................................

PHONE: ..........................................................................

EMAIL: ..........................................................................

NAME: ............................................................................

ADDRESS: ........................................................................

............................................................................

............................................................................

PHONE: ..........................................................................

EMAIL: ..........................................................................

NAME: ............................................................................

ADDRESS: ........................................................................

............................................................................

............................................................................

PHONE: ..........................................................................

EMAIL: ..........................................................................

NAME: ............................................................................

ADDRESS: ........................................................................

............................................................................

............................................................................

PHONE: ..........................................................................

EMAIL: ..........................................................................

NAME:
ADDRESS:

PHONE:
EMAIL:

NAME:
ADDRESS:

PHONE:
EMAIL:

NAME:
ADDRESS:

PHONE:
EMAIL:

NAME:
ADDRESS:

PHONE:
EMAIL:

NAME:
ADDRESS:

PHONE:
EMAIL:

# BIRTHDAYS

## DON'T FORGET YOUR NAN/BROTHER/DOG/CAT, ETC, ETC.

### JANUARY

WHO . . . . . . . . . . . . . . . . . . . . . . . . . . WHEN . . . . . . . . . . . . . . . . . . . . . . . . . . . . . . . .
WHO . . . . . . . . . . . . . . . . . . . . . . . . . . WHEN . . . . . . . . . . . . . . . . . . . . . . . . . . . . . . . .
WHO . . . . . . . . . . . . . . . . . . . . . . . . . . WHEN . . . . . . . . . . . . . . . . . . . . . . . . . . . . . . . .

WHO . . . . . . . . . . . . . . . . . . . . . . . . . . WHEN . . . . . . . . . . . . . . . . . . . . . . . . . . . . . . . .
WHO . . . . . . . . . . . . . . . . . . . . . . . . . . WHEN . . . . . . . . . . . . . . . . . . . . . . . . . . . . . . . .
WHO . . . . . . . . . . . . . . . . . . . . . . . . . . WHEN . . . . . . . . . . . . . . . . . . . . . . . . . . . . . . . .
WHO . . . . . . . . . . . . . . . . . . . . . . . . . . WHEN . . . . . . . . . . . . . . . . . . . . . . . . . . . . . . . .
WHO . . . . . . . . . . . . . . . . . . . . . . . . . . WHEN . . . . . . . . . . . . . . . . . . . . . . . . . . . . . . . .
WHO . . . . . . . . . . . . . . . . . . . . . . . . . . WHEN . . . . . . . . . . . . . . . . . . . . . . . . . . . . . . . .

### FEBRUARY

WHO . . . . . . . . . . . . . . . . . . . . . . . . . . WHEN . . . . . . . . . . . . . . . . . . . . . . . . . . . . . . . .
WHO . . . . . . . . . . . . . . . . . . . . . . . . . . WHEN . . . . . . . . . . . . . . . . . . . . . . . . . . . . . . . .
WHO . . . . . . . . . . . . . . . . . . . . . . . . . . WHEN . . . . . . . . . . . . . . . . . . . . . . . . . . . . . . . .
WHO . . . . . . . . . . . . . . . . . . . . . . . . . . WHEN . . . . . . . . . . . . . . . . . . . . . . . . . . . . . . . .
WHO . . . . . . . . . . . . . . . . . . . . . . . . . . WHEN . . . . . . . . . . . . . . . . . . . . . . . . . . . . . . . .
WHO . . . . . . . . . . . . . . . . . . . . . . . . . . WHEN . . . . . . . . . . . . . . . . . . . . . . . . . . . . . . . .
WHO . . . . . . . . . . . . . . . . . . . . . . . . . . WHEN . . . . . . . . . . . . . . . . . . . . . . . . . . . . . . . .
WHO . . . . . . . . . . . . . . . . . . . . . . . . . . WHEN . . . . . . . . . . . . . . . . . . . . . . . . . . . . . . . .
WHO . . . . . . . . . . . . . . . . . . . . . . . . . . WHEN . . . . . . . . . . . . . . . . . . . . . . . . . . . . . . . .

### MARCH

WHO . . . . . . . . . . . . . . . . . . . . . . . . . . WHEN . . . . . . . . . . . . . . . . . . . . . . . . . . . . . . . .
WHO . . . . . . . . . . . . . . . . . . . . . . . . . . WHEN . . . . . . . . . . . . . . . . . . . . . . . . . . . . . . . .
WHO . . . . . . . . . . . . . . . . . . . . . . . . . . WHEN . . . . . . . . . . . . . . . . . . . . . . . . . . . . . . . .
WHO . . . . . . . . . . . . . . . . . . . . . . . . . . WHEN . . . . . . . . . . . . . . . . . . . . . . . . . . . . . . . .
WHO . . . . . . . . . . . . . . . . . . . . . . . . . . WHEN . . . . . . . . . . . . . . . . . . . . . . . . . . . . . . . .
WHO . . . . . . . . . . . . . . . . . . . . . . . . . . WHEN . . . . . . . . . . . . . . . . . . . . . . . . . . . . . . . .
WHO . . . . . . . . . . . . . . . . . . . . . . . . . . WHEN . . . . . . . . . . . . . . . . . . . . . . . . . . . . . . . .
WHO . . . . . . . . . . . . . . . . . . . . . . . . . . WHEN . . . . . . . . . . . . . . . . . . . . . . . . . . . . . . . .
WHO . . . . . . . . . . . . . . . . . . . . . . . . . . WHEN . . . . . . . . . . . . . . . . . . . . . . . . . . . . . . . .

# DON'T FORGET YOUR NAN/BROTHER/DOG/CAT, ETC, ETC.

## APRIL

WHO . . . . . . . . . . . . . . . . . . . . . . . . . . . WHEN . . . . . . . . . . . . . . . . . . . . . . . . . . . . . .
WHO . . . . . . . . . . . . . . . . . . . . . . . . . . . WHEN . . . . . . . . . . . . . . . . . . . . . . . . . . . . . .
WHO . . . . . . . . . . . . . . . . . . . . . . . . . . . WHEN . . . . . . . . . . . . . . . . . . . . . . . . . . . . . .
WHO . . . . . . . . . . . . . . . . . . . . . . . . . . . WHEN . . . . . . . . . . . . . . . . . . . . . . . . . . . . . .
WHO . . . . . . . . . . . . . . . . . . . . . . . . . . . WHEN . . . . . . . . . . . . . . . . . . . . . . . . . . . . . .
WHO . . . . . . . . . . . . . . . . . . . . . . . . . . . WHEN . . . . . . . . . . . . . . . . . . . . . . . . . . . . . .
WHO . . . . . . . . . . . . . . . . . . . . . . . . . . . WHEN . . . . . . . . . . . . . . . . . . . . . . . . . . . . . .
WHO . . . . . . . . . . . . . . . . . . . . . . . . . . . WHEN . . . . . . . . . . . . . . . . . . . . . . . . . . . . . .
WHO . . . . . . . . . . . . . . . . . . . . . . . . . . . WHEN . . . . . . . . . . . . . . . . . . . . . . . . . . . . . .

## MAY

WHO . . . . . . . . . . . . . . . . . . . . . . . . . . . WHEN . . . . . . . . . . . . . . . . . . . . . . . . . . . . . .
WHO . . . . . . . . . . . . . . . . . . . . . . . . . . . WHEN . . . . . . . . . . . . . . . . . . . . . . . . . . . . . .
WHO . . . . . . . . . . . . . . . . . . . . . . . . . . . WHEN . . . . . . . . . . . . . . . . . . . . . . . . . . . . . .
WHO . . . . . . . . . . . . . . . . . . . . . . . . . . . WHEN . . . . . . . . . . . . . . . . . . . . . . . . . . . . . .
WHO . . . . . . . . . . . . . . . . . . . . . . . . . . . WHEN . . . . . . . . . . . . . . . . . . . . . . . . . . . . . .
WHO . . . . . . . . . . . . . . . . . . . . . . . . . . . WHEN . . . . . . . . . . . . . . . . . . . . . . . . . . . . . .
WHO . . . . . . . . . . . . . . . . . . . . . . . . . . . WHEN . . . . . . . . . . . . . . . . . . . . . . . . . . . . . .
WHO . . . . . . . . . . . . . . . . . . . . . . . . . . . WHEN . . . . . . . . . . . . . . . . . . . . . . . . . . . . . .
WHO . . . . . . . . . . . . . . . . . . . . . . . . . . . WHEN . . . . . . . . . . . . . . . . . . . . . . . . . . . . . .

## JUNE

WHO . . . . . . . . . . . . . . . . . . . . . . . . . . . WHEN . . . . . . . . . . . . . . . . . . . . . . . . . . . . . .
WHO . . . . . . . . . . . . . . . . . . . . . . . . . . . WHEN . . . . . . . . . . . . . . . . . . . . . . . . . . . . . .
WHO . . . . . . . . . . . . . . . . . . . . . . . . . . . WHEN . . . . . . . . . . . . . . . . . . . . . . . . . . . . . .
WHO . . . . . . . . . . . . . . . . . . . . . . . . . . . WHEN . . . . . . . . . . . . . . . . . . . . . . . . . . . . . .
WHO . . . . . . . . . . . . . . . . . . . . . . . . . . . WHEN . . . . . . . . . . . . . . . . . . . . . . . . . . . . . .
WHO . . . . . . . . . . . . . . . . . . . . . . . . . . . WHEN . . . . . . . . . . . . . . . . . . . . . . . . . . . . . .
WHO . . . . . . . . . . . . . . . . . . . . . . . . . . . WHEN . . . . . . . . . . . . . . . . . . . . . . . . . . . . . .
WHO . . . . . . . . . . . . . . . . . . . . . . . . . . . WHEN . . . . . . . . . . . . . . . . . . . . . . . . . . . . . .
WHO . . . . . . . . . . . . . . . . . . . . . . . . . . . WHEN . . . . . . . . . . . . . . . . . . . . . . . . . . . . . .

# BIRTHDAYS

## DON'T FORGET YOUR NAN/BROTHER/DOG/CAT, ETC, ETC.

### JULY

WHO . . . . . . . . . . . . . . . . . . . . . . . . . . . . WHEN . . . . . . . . . . . . . . . . . . . . . . . . . . . .
WHO . . . . . . . . . . . . . . . . . . . . . . . . . . . . WHEN . . . . . . . . . . . . . . . . . . . . . . . . . . . .
WHO . . . . . . . . . . . . . . . . . . . . . . . . . . . . WHEN . . . . . . . . . . . . . . . . . . . . . . . . . . . .
WHO . . . . . . . . . . . . . . . . . . . . . . . . . . . . WHEN . . . . . . . . . . . . . . . . . . . . . . . . . . . .
WHO . . . . . . . . . . . . . . . . . . . . . . . . . . . . WHEN . . . . . . . . . . . . . . . . . . . . . . . . . . . .
WHO . . . . . . . . . . . . . . . . . . . . . . . . . . . . WHEN . . . . . . . . . . . . . . . . . . . . . . . . . . . .
WHO . . . . . . . . . . . . . . . . . . . . . . . . . . . . WHEN . . . . . . . . . . . . . . . . . . . . . . . . . . . .
WHO . . . . . . . . . . . . . . . . . . . . . . . . . . . . WHEN . . . . . . . . . . . . . . . . . . . . . . . . . . . .
WHO . . . . . . . . . . . . . . . . . . . . . . . . . . . . WHEN . . . . . . . . . . . . . . . . . . . . . . . . . . . .

### AUGUST

WHO . . . . . . . . . . . . . . . . . . . . . . . . . . . . WHEN . . . . . . . . . . . . . . . . . . . . . . . . . . . .
WHO . . . . . . . . . . . . . . . . . . . . . . . . . . . . WHEN . . . . . . . . . . . . . . . . . . . . . . . . . . . .
WHO . . . . . . . . . . . . . . . . . . . . . . . . . . . . WHEN . . . . . . . . . . . . . . . . . . . . . . . . . . . .
WHO . . . . . . . . . . . . . . . . . . . . . . . . . . . . WHEN . . . . . . . . . . . . . . . . . . . . . . . . . . . .
WHO . . . . . . . . . . . . . . . . . . . . . . . . . . . . WHEN . . . . . . . . . . . . . . . . . . . . . . . . . . . .
WHO . . . . . . . . . . . . . . . . . . . . . . . . . . . . WHEN . . . . . . . . . . . . . . . . . . . . . . . . . . . .
WHO . . . . . . . . . . . . . . . . . . . . . . . . . . . . WHEN . . . . . . . . . . . . . . . . . . . . . . . . . . . .
WHO . . . . . . . . . . . . . . . . . . . . . . . . . . . . WHEN . . . . . . . . . . . . . . . . . . . . . . . . . . . .
WHO . . . . . . . . . . . . . . . . . . . . . . . . . . . . WHEN . . . . . . . . . . . . . . . . . . . . . . . . . . . .

### SEPTEMBER

WHO . . . . . . . . . . . . . . . . . . . . . . . . . . . . WHEN . . . . . . . . . . . . . . . . . . . . . . . . . . . .
WHO . . . . . . . . . . . . . . . . . . . . . . . . . . . . WHEN . . . . . . . . . . . . . . . . . . . . . . . . . . . .
WHO . . . . . . . . . . . . . . . . . . . . . . . . . . . . WHEN . . . . . . . . . . . . . . . . . . . . . . . . . . . .
WHO . . . . . . . . . . . . . . . . . . . . . . . . . . . . WHEN . . . . . . . . . . . . . . . . . . . . . . . . . . . .
WHO . . . . . . . . . . . . . . . . . . . . . . . . . . . . WHEN . . . . . . . . . . . . . . . . . . . . . . . . . . . .
WHO . . . . . . . . . . . . . . . . . . . . . . . . . . . . WHEN . . . . . . . . . . . . . . . . . . . . . . . . . . . .
WHO . . . . . . . . . . . . . . . . . . . . . . . . . . . . WHEN . . . . . . . . . . . . . . . . . . . . . . . . . . . .
WHO . . . . . . . . . . . . . . . . . . . . . . . . . . . . WHEN . . . . . . . . . . . . . . . . . . . . . . . . . . . .
WHO . . . . . . . . . . . . . . . . . . . . . . . . . . . . WHEN . . . . . . . . . . . . . . . . . . . . . . . . . . . .

●●●

# DON'T FORGET YOUR NAN/BROTHER/DOG/CAT, ETC, ETC.

## OCTOBER

WHO . . . . . . . . . . . . . . . . . . . . . . . . . . . . . WHEN . . . . . . . . . . . . . . . . . . . . . . . . . . . . .
WHO . . . . . . . . . . . . . . . . . . . . . . . . . . . . . WHEN . . . . . . . . . . . . . . . . . . . . . . . . . . . . .
WHO . . . . . . . . . . . . . . . . . . . . . . . . . . . . . WHEN . . . . . . . . . . . . . . . . . . . . . . . . . . . . .
WHO . . . . . . . . . . . . . . . . . . . . . . . . . . . . . WHEN . . . . . . . . . . . . . . . . . . . . . . . . . . . . .
WHO . . . . . . . . . . . . . . . . . . . . . . . . . . . . . WHEN . . . . . . . . . . . . . . . . . . . . . . . . . . . . .
WHO . . . . . . . . . . . . . . . . . . . . . . . . . . . . . WHEN . . . . . . . . . . . . . . . . . . . . . . . . . . . . .
WHO . . . . . . . . . . . . . . . . . . . . . . . . . . . . . WHEN . . . . . . . . . . . . . . . . . . . . . . . . . . . . .
WHO . . . . . . . . . . . . . . . . . . . . . . . . . . . . . WHEN . . . . . . . . . . . . . . . . . . . . . . . . . . . . .
WHO . . . . . . . . . . . . . . . . . . . . . . . . . . . . . WHEN . . . . . . . . . . . . . . . . . . . . . . . . . . . . .

## NOVEMBER

WHO . . . . . . . . . . . . . . . . . . . . . . . . . . . . . WHEN . . . . . . . . . . . . . . . . . . . . . . . . . . . . .
WHO . . . . . . . . . . . . . . . . . . . . . . . . . . . . . WHEN . . . . . . . . . . . . . . . . . . . . . . . . . . . . .
WHO . . . . . . . . . . . . . . . . . . . . . . . . . . . . . WHEN . . . . . . . . . . . . . . . . . . . . . . . . . . . . .
WHO . . . . . . . . . . . . . . . . . . . . . . . . . . . . . WHEN . . . . . . . . . . . . . . . . . . . . . . . . . . . . .
WHO . . . . . . . . . . . . . . . . . . . . . . . . . . . . . WHEN . . . . . . . . . . . . . . . . . . . . . . . . . . . . .
WHO . . . . . . . . . . . . . . . . . . . . . . . . . . . . . WHEN . . . . . . . . . . . . . . . . . . . . . . . . . . . . .
WHO . . . . . . . . . . . . . . . . . . . . . . . . . . . . . WHEN . . . . . . . . . . . . . . . . . . . . . . . . . . . . .
WHO . . . . . . . . . . . . . . . . . . . . . . . . . . . . . WHEN . . . . . . . . . . . . . . . . . . . . . . . . . . . . .
WHO . . . . . . . . . . . . . . . . . . . . . . . . . . . . . WHEN . . . . . . . . . . . . . . . . . . . . . . . . . . . . .

## DECEMBER

WHO . . . . . . . . . . . . . . . . . . . . . . . . . . . . . WHEN . . . . . . . . . . . . . . . . . . . . . . . . . . . . .
WHO . . . . . . . . . . . . . . . . . . . . . . . . . . . . . WHEN . . . . . . . . . . . . . . . . . . . . . . . . . . . . .
WHO . . . . . . . . . . . . . . . . . . . . . . . . . . . . . WHEN . . . . . . . . . . . . . . . . . . . . . . . . . . . . .
WHO . . . . . . . . . . . . . . . . . . . . . . . . . . . . . WHEN . . . . . . . . . . . . . . . . . . . . . . . . . . . . .
WHO . . . . . . . . . . . . . . . . . . . . . . . . . . . . . WHEN . . . . . . . . . . . . . . . . . . . . . . . . . . . . .
WHO . . . . . . . . . . . . . . . . . . . . . . . . . . . . . WHEN . . . . . . . . . . . . . . . . . . . . . . . . . . . . .
WHO . . . . . . . . . . . . . . . . . . . . . . . . . . . . . WHEN . . . . . . . . . . . . . . . . . . . . . . . . . . . . .
WHO . . . . . . . . . . . . . . . . . . . . . . . . . . . . . WHEN . . . . . . . . . . . . . . . . . . . . . . . . . . . . .
WHO . . . . . . . . . . . . . . . . . . . . . . . . . . . . . WHEN . . . . . . . . . . . . . . . . . . . . . . . . . . . . .

# GIFT IDEAS

BIRTHDAYS AND CHRISTMAS CAN CREEP UP ON YOU. DON'T LEAVE IT 'TIL THE DAY BEFORE. IF YOU SEE AN IDEA, JOT IT DOWN, MAKES YOU LOOK FABULOUS WHEN YOU GIVE BIG COUSIN DAISY SOMETHING SHE ADORED 6 MONTHS AGO!

USE A PENCIL SO YOU CAN RUB IT OUT AND USE IT AGAIN

# MONEY IN

## STUDENT LOANS AND GRANTS

### YEAR 1

**TERM 1**

AMOUNT: .................................. DATE: .............................................

AMOUNT: .................................. DATE: .............................................

AMOUNT: .................................. DATE: .............................................

AMOUNT: .................................. DATE: .............................................

AMOUNT: .................................. DATE: .............................................

**TERM 2**

AMOUNT: .................................. DATE: .............................................

AMOUNT: .................................. DATE: .............................................

AMOUNT: .................................. DATE: .............................................

AMOUNT: .................................. DATE: .............................................

AMOUNT: .................................. DATE: .............................................

**TERM 3**

AMOUNT: .................................. DATE: .............................................

AMOUNT: .................................. DATE: .............................................

AMOUNT: .................................. DATE: .............................................

AMOUNT: .................................. DATE: .............................................

AMOUNT: .................................. DATE: .............................................

● ● ●

# MONEY OUT

## ACCOMMODATION, ETC.

**YEAR 1**

### TERM 1

AMOUNT: . . . . . . . . . . . . . . . . . . . . . DATE: . . . . . . . . . . . . . . . . . . . . . . . . . . . . . . . . .

AMOUNT: . . . . . . . . . . . . . . . . . . . . . DATE: . . . . . . . . . . . . . . . . . . . . . . . . . . . . . . . . .

AMOUNT: . . . . . . . . . . . . . . . . . . . . . DATE: . . . . . . . . . . . . . . . . . . . . . . . . . . . . . . . . .

AMOUNT: . . . . . . . . . . . . . . . . . . . . . DATE: . . . . . . . . . . . . . . . . . . . . . . . . . . . . . . . . .

AMOUNT: . . . . . . . . . . . . . . . . . . . . . DATE: . . . . . . . . . . . . . . . . . . . . . . . . . . . . . . . . .

### TERM 2

AMOUNT: . . . . . . . . . . . . . . . . . . . . . DATE: . . . . . . . . . . . . . . . . . . . . . . . . . . . . . . . . .

AMOUNT: . . . . . . . . . . . . . . . . . . . . . DATE: . . . . . . . . . . . . . . . . . . . . . . . . . . . . . . . . .

AMOUNT: . . . . . . . . . . . . . . . . . . . . . DATE: . . . . . . . . . . . . . . . . . . . . . . . . . . . . . . . . .

AMOUNT: . . . . . . . . . . . . . . . . . . . . . DATE: . . . . . . . . . . . . . . . . . . . . . . . . . . . . . . . . .

AMOUNT: . . . . . . . . . . . . . . . . . . . . . DATE: . . . . . . . . . . . . . . . . . . . . . . . . . . . . . . . . .

### TERM 3

AMOUNT: . . . . . . . . . . . . . . . . . . . . . DATE: . . . . . . . . . . . . . . . . . . . . . . . . . . . . . . . . .

AMOUNT: . . . . . . . . . . . . . . . . . . . . . DATE: . . . . . . . . . . . . . . . . . . . . . . . . . . . . . . . . .

AMOUNT: . . . . . . . . . . . . . . . . . . . . . DATE: . . . . . . . . . . . . . . . . . . . . . . . . . . . . . . . . .

AMOUNT: . . . . . . . . . . . . . . . . . . . . . DATE: . . . . . . . . . . . . . . . . . . . . . . . . . . . . . . . . .

AMOUNT: . . . . . . . . . . . . . . . . . . . . . DATE: . . . . . . . . . . . . . . . . . . . . . . . . . . . . . . . . .

— ••• —

# WORKING OUT PAGES

# MONEY IN

## STUDENT LOANS AND GRANTS

### YEAR 2

**TERM 1**

AMOUNT: . . . . . . . . . . . . . . . . . . . . . . . DATE: . . . . . . . . . . . . . . . . . . . . . . . . . . . . . . . . . . . . . . . . . .

AMOUNT: . . . . . . . . . . . . . . . . . . . . . . . DATE: . . . . . . . . . . . . . . . . . . . . . . . . . . . . . . . . . . . . . . . . . .

AMOUNT: . . . . . . . . . . . . . . . . . . . . . . . DATE: . . . . . . . . . . . . . . . . . . . . . . . . . . . . . . . . . . . . . . . . . .

AMOUNT: . . . . . . . . . . . . . . . . . . . . . . . DATE: . . . . . . . . . . . . . . . . . . . . . . . . . . . . . . . . . . . . . . . . . .

AMOUNT: . . . . . . . . . . . . . . . . . . . . . . . DATE: . . . . . . . . . . . . . . . . . . . . . . . . . . . . . . . . . . . . . . . . . .

**TERM 2**

AMOUNT: . . . . . . . . . . . . . . . . . . . . . . . DATE: . . . . . . . . . . . . . . . . . . . . . . . . . . . . . . . . . . . . . . . . . .

AMOUNT: . . . . . . . . . . . . . . . . . . . . . . . DATE: . . . . . . . . . . . . . . . . . . . . . . . . . . . . . . . . . . . . . . . . . .

AMOUNT: . . . . . . . . . . . . . . . . . . . . . . . DATE: . . . . . . . . . . . . . . . . . . . . . . . . . . . . . . . . . . . . . . . . . .

AMOUNT: . . . . . . . . . . . . . . . . . . . . . . . DATE: . . . . . . . . . . . . . . . . . . . . . . . . . . . . . . . . . . . . . . . . . .

AMOUNT: . . . . . . . . . . . . . . . . . . . . . . . DATE: . . . . . . . . . . . . . . . . . . . . . . . . . . . . . . . . . . . . . . . . . .

**TERM 3**

AMOUNT: . . . . . . . . . . . . . . . . . . . . . . . DATE: . . . . . . . . . . . . . . . . . . . . . . . . . . . . . . . . . . . . . . . . . .

AMOUNT: . . . . . . . . . . . . . . . . . . . . . . . DATE: . . . . . . . . . . . . . . . . . . . . . . . . . . . . . . . . . . . . . . . . . .

AMOUNT: . . . . . . . . . . . . . . . . . . . . . . . DATE: . . . . . . . . . . . . . . . . . . . . . . . . . . . . . . . . . . . . . . . . . .

AMOUNT: . . . . . . . . . . . . . . . . . . . . . . . DATE: . . . . . . . . . . . . . . . . . . . . . . . . . . . . . . . . . . . . . . . . . .

AMOUNT: . . . . . . . . . . . . . . . . . . . . . . . DATE: . . . . . . . . . . . . . . . . . . . . . . . . . . . . . . . . . . . . . . . . . .

● ● ●

# MONEY OUT

## ACCOMMODATION, ETC.

**YEAR 2**

### TERM 1

AMOUNT: . . . . . . . . . . . . . . . . . . . . . . . . DATE: . . . . . . . . . . . . . . . . . . . . . . . . . . . . . . . . . . . . . . . . .

AMOUNT: . . . . . . . . . . . . . . . . . . . . . . . . DATE: . . . . . . . . . . . . . . . . . . . . . . . . . . . . . . . . . . . . . . . . .

AMOUNT: . . . . . . . . . . . . . . . . . . . . . . . . DATE: . . . . . . . . . . . . . . . . . . . . . . . . . . . . . . . . . . . . . . . . .

AMOUNT: . . . . . . . . . . . . . . . . . . . . . . . . DATE: . . . . . . . . . . . . . . . . . . . . . . . . . . . . . . . . . . . . . . . . .

AMOUNT: . . . . . . . . . . . . . . . . . . . . . . . . DATE: . . . . . . . . . . . . . . . . . . . . . . . . . . . . . . . . . . . . . . . . .

### TERM 2

AMOUNT: . . . . . . . . . . . . . . . . . . . . . . . . DATE: . . . . . . . . . . . . . . . . . . . . . . . . . . . . . . . . . . . . . . . . .

AMOUNT: . . . . . . . . . . . . . . . . . . . . . . . . DATE: . . . . . . . . . . . . . . . . . . . . . . . . . . . . . . . . . . . . . . . . .

AMOUNT: . . . . . . . . . . . . . . . . . . . . . . . . DATE: . . . . . . . . . . . . . . . . . . . . . . . . . . . . . . . . . . . . . . . . .

AMOUNT: . . . . . . . . . . . . . . . . . . . . . . . . DATE: . . . . . . . . . . . . . . . . . . . . . . . . . . . . . . . . . . . . . . . . .

AMOUNT: . . . . . . . . . . . . . . . . . . . . . . . . DATE: . . . . . . . . . . . . . . . . . . . . . . . . . . . . . . . . . . . . . . . . .

### TERM 3

AMOUNT: . . . . . . . . . . . . . . . . . . . . . . . . DATE: . . . . . . . . . . . . . . . . . . . . . . . . . . . . . . . . . . . . . . . . .

AMOUNT: . . . . . . . . . . . . . . . . . . . . . . . . DATE: . . . . . . . . . . . . . . . . . . . . . . . . . . . . . . . . . . . . . . . . .

AMOUNT: . . . . . . . . . . . . . . . . . . . . . . . . DATE: . . . . . . . . . . . . . . . . . . . . . . . . . . . . . . . . . . . . . . . . .

AMOUNT: . . . . . . . . . . . . . . . . . . . . . . . . DATE: . . . . . . . . . . . . . . . . . . . . . . . . . . . . . . . . . . . . . . . . .

AMOUNT: . . . . . . . . . . . . . . . . . . . . . . . . DATE: . . . . . . . . . . . . . . . . . . . . . . . . . . . . . . . . . . . . . . . . .

— ● ● ● —

# WORKING OUT PAGES

# MONEY IN

## STUDENT LOANS AND GRANTS

### YEAR 3

**TERM 1**

AMOUNT: .......................... DATE: ........................................

AMOUNT: .......................... DATE: ........................................

AMOUNT: .......................... DATE: ........................................

AMOUNT: .......................... DATE: ........................................

AMOUNT: .......................... DATE: ........................................

**TERM 2**

AMOUNT: .......................... DATE: ........................................

AMOUNT: .......................... DATE: ........................................

AMOUNT: .......................... DATE: ........................................

AMOUNT: .......................... DATE: ........................................

AMOUNT: .......................... DATE: ........................................

**TERM 3**

AMOUNT: .......................... DATE: ........................................

AMOUNT: .......................... DATE: ........................................

AMOUNT: .......................... DATE: ........................................

AMOUNT: .......................... DATE: ........................................

AMOUNT: .......................... DATE: ........................................

# MONEY OUT

## ACCOMMODATION, ETC.

**YEAR 3**

### TERM 1

AMOUNT: . . . . . . . . . . . . . . . . DATE: . . . . . . . . . . . . . . . . . . . . . . . . . . . . . . . . .

AMOUNT: . . . . . . . . . . . . . . . . DATE: . . . . . . . . . . . . . . . . . . . . . . . . . . . . . . . . .

AMOUNT: . . . . . . . . . . . . . . . . DATE: . . . . . . . . . . . . . . . . . . . . . . . . . . . . . . . . .

AMOUNT: . . . . . . . . . . . . . . . . DATE: . . . . . . . . . . . . . . . . . . . . . . . . . . . . . . . . .

AMOUNT: . . . . . . . . . . . . . . . . DATE: . . . . . . . . . . . . . . . . . . . . . . . . . . . . . . . . .

### TERM 2

AMOUNT: . . . . . . . . . . . . . . . . DATE: . . . . . . . . . . . . . . . . . . . . . . . . . . . . . . . . .

AMOUNT: . . . . . . . . . . . . . . . . DATE: . . . . . . . . . . . . . . . . . . . . . . . . . . . . . . . . .

AMOUNT: . . . . . . . . . . . . . . . . DATE: . . . . . . . . . . . . . . . . . . . . . . . . . . . . . . . . .

AMOUNT: . . . . . . . . . . . . . . . . DATE: . . . . . . . . . . . . . . . . . . . . . . . . . . . . . . . . .

AMOUNT: . . . . . . . . . . . . . . . . DATE: . . . . . . . . . . . . . . . . . . . . . . . . . . . . . . . . .

### TERM 3

AMOUNT: . . . . . . . . . . . . . . . . DATE: . . . . . . . . . . . . . . . . . . . . . . . . . . . . . . . . .

AMOUNT: . . . . . . . . . . . . . . . . DATE: . . . . . . . . . . . . . . . . . . . . . . . . . . . . . . . . .

AMOUNT: . . . . . . . . . . . . . . . . DATE: . . . . . . . . . . . . . . . . . . . . . . . . . . . . . . . . .

AMOUNT: . . . . . . . . . . . . . . . . DATE: . . . . . . . . . . . . . . . . . . . . . . . . . . . . . . . . .

AMOUNT: . . . . . . . . . . . . . . . . DATE: . . . . . . . . . . . . . . . . . . . . . . . . . . . . . . . . .

# WORKING OUT PAGES

# FUTURE PLANS AFTER UNI

# FUTURE PLANS AFTER UNI

# CALENDAR YEAR 1

## JAN

| | | | | | | |
|---|---|---|---|---|---|---|
| 1 | 2 | 3 | 4 | 5 | 6 | 7 |
| 8 | 9 | 10 | 11 | 12 | 13 | 14 |
| 15 | 16 | 17 | 18 | 19 | 20 | 21 |
| 22 | 23 | 24 | 25 | 26 | 27 | 28 |
| 29 | 30 | 31 | | | | |

## FEB

| | | | | | | |
|---|---|---|---|---|---|---|
| 1 | 2 | 3 | 4 | 5 | 6 | 7 |
| 8 | 9 | 10 | 11 | 12 | 13 | 14 |
| 15 | 16 | 17 | 18 | 19 | 20 | 21 |
| 22 | 23 | 24 | 25 | 26 | 27 | 28 |
| 29 | | | | | | |

## MAR

| | | | | | | |
|---|---|---|---|---|---|---|
| 1 | 2 | 3 | 4 | 5 | 6 | 7 |
| 8 | 9 | 10 | 11 | 12 | 13 | 14 |
| 15 | 16 | 17 | 18 | 19 | 20 | 21 |
| 22 | 23 | 24 | 25 | 26 | 27 | 28 |
| 29 | 30 | 31 | | | | |

## APR

| | | | | | | |
|---|---|---|---|---|---|---|
| 1 | 2 | 3 | 4 | 5 | 6 | 7 |
| 8 | 9 | 10 | 11 | 12 | 13 | 14 |
| 15 | 16 | 17 | 18 | 19 | 20 | 21 |
| 22 | 23 | 24 | 25 | 26 | 27 | 28 |
| 29 | 30 | | | | | |

## MAY

| | | | | | | |
|---|---|---|---|---|---|---|
| 1 | 2 | 3 | 4 | 5 | 6 | 7 |
| 8 | 9 | 10 | 11 | 12 | 13 | 14 |
| 15 | 16 | 17 | 18 | 19 | 20 | 21 |
| 22 | 23 | 24 | 25 | 26 | 27 | 28 |
| 29 | 30 | 31 | | | | |

## JUN

| | | | | | | |
|---|---|---|---|---|---|---|
| 1 | 2 | 3 | 4 | 5 | 6 | 7 |
| 8 | 9 | 10 | 11 | 12 | 13 | 14 |
| 15 | 16 | 17 | 18 | 19 | 20 | 21 |
| 22 | 23 | 24 | 25 | 26 | 27 | 28 |
| 29 | 30 | | | | | |

## JUL

| | | | | | | |
|---|---|---|---|---|---|---|
| 1 | 2 | 3 | 4 | 5 | 6 | 7 |
| 8 | 9 | 10 | 11 | 12 | 13 | 14 |
| 15 | 16 | 17 | 18 | 19 | 20 | 21 |
| 22 | 23 | 24 | 25 | 26 | 27 | 28 |
| 29 | 30 | 31 | | | | |

## AUG

| | | | | | | |
|---|---|---|---|---|---|---|
| 1 | 2 | 3 | 4 | 5 | 6 | 7 |
| 8 | 9 | 10 | 11 | 12 | 13 | 14 |
| 15 | 16 | 17 | 18 | 19 | 20 | 21 |
| 22 | 23 | 24 | 25 | 26 | 27 | 28 |
| 29 | 30 | 31 | | | | |

## SEPT

| | | | | | | |
|---|---|---|---|---|---|---|
| 1 | 2 | 3 | 4 | 5 | 6 | 7 |
| 8 | 9 | 10 | 11 | 12 | 13 | 14 |
| 15 | 16 | 17 | 18 | 19 | 20 | 21 |
| 22 | 23 | 24 | 25 | 26 | 27 | 28 |
| 29 | 30 | | | | | |

## OCT

| | | | | | | |
|---|---|---|---|---|---|---|
| 1 | 2 | 3 | 4 | 5 | 6 | 7 |
| 8 | 9 | 10 | 11 | 12 | 13 | 14 |
| 15 | 16 | 17 | 18 | 19 | 20 | 21 |
| 22 | 23 | 24 | 25 | 26 | 27 | 28 |
| 29 | 30 | 31 | | | | |

## NOV

| | | | | | | |
|---|---|---|---|---|---|---|
| 1 | 2 | 3 | 4 | 5 | 6 | 7 |
| 8 | 9 | 10 | 11 | 12 | 13 | 14 |
| 15 | 16 | 17 | 18 | 19 | 20 | 21 |
| 22 | 23 | 24 | 25 | 26 | 27 | 28 |
| 29 | 30 | | | | | |

## DEC

| | | | | | | |
|---|---|---|---|---|---|---|
| 1 | 2 | 3 | 4 | 5 | 6 | 7 |
| 8 | 9 | 10 | 11 | 12 | 13 | 14 |
| 15 | 16 | 17 | 18 | 19 | 20 | 21 |
| 22 | 23 | 24 | 25 | 26 | 27 | 28 |
| 29 | 30 | 31 | | | | |

# CALENDAR YEAR 2

## JAN

| | | | | | | |
|---|---|---|---|---|---|---|
| 1 | 2 | 3 | 4 | 5 | 6 | 7 |
| 8 | 9 | 10 | 11 | 12 | 13 | 14 |
| 15 | 16 | 17 | 18 | 19 | 20 | 21 |
| 22 | 23 | 24 | 25 | 26 | 27 | 28 |
| 29 | 30 | 31 | | | | |

## FEB

| | | | | | | |
|---|---|---|---|---|---|---|
| 1 | 2 | 3 | 4 | 5 | 6 | 7 |
| 8 | 9 | 10 | 11 | 12 | 13 | 14 |
| 15 | 16 | 17 | 18 | 19 | 20 | 21 |
| 22 | 23 | 24 | 25 | 26 | 27 | 28 |
| 29 | | | | | | |

## MAR

| | | | | | | |
|---|---|---|---|---|---|---|
| 1 | 2 | 3 | 4 | 5 | 6 | 7 |
| 8 | 9 | 10 | 11 | 12 | 13 | 14 |
| 15 | 16 | 17 | 18 | 19 | 20 | 21 |
| 22 | 23 | 24 | 25 | 26 | 27 | 28 |
| 29 | 30 | 31 | | | | |

## APR

| | | | | | | |
|---|---|---|---|---|---|---|
| 1 | 2 | 3 | 4 | 5 | 6 | 7 |
| 8 | 9 | 10 | 11 | 12 | 13 | 14 |
| 15 | 16 | 17 | 18 | 19 | 20 | 21 |
| 22 | 23 | 24 | 25 | 26 | 27 | 28 |
| 29 | 30 | | | | | |

## MAY

| | | | | | | |
|---|---|---|---|---|---|---|
| 1 | 2 | 3 | 4 | 5 | 6 | 7 |
| 8 | 9 | 10 | 11 | 12 | 13 | 14 |
| 15 | 16 | 17 | 18 | 19 | 20 | 21 |
| 22 | 23 | 24 | 25 | 26 | 27 | 28 |
| 29 | 30 | 31 | | | | |

## JUN

| | | | | | | |
|---|---|---|---|---|---|---|
| 1 | 2 | 3 | 4 | 5 | 6 | 7 |
| 8 | 9 | 10 | 11 | 12 | 13 | 14 |
| 15 | 16 | 17 | 18 | 19 | 20 | 21 |
| 22 | 23 | 24 | 25 | 26 | 27 | 28 |
| 29 | 30 | | | | | |

## JUL

| | | | | | | |
|---|---|---|---|---|---|---|
| 1 | 2 | 3 | 4 | 5 | 6 | 7 |
| 8 | 9 | 10 | 11 | 12 | 13 | 14 |
| 15 | 16 | 17 | 18 | 19 | 20 | 21 |
| 22 | 23 | 24 | 25 | 26 | 27 | 28 |
| 29 | 30 | 31 | | | | |

## AUG

| | | | | | | |
|---|---|---|---|---|---|---|
| 1 | 2 | 3 | 4 | 5 | 6 | 7 |
| 8 | 9 | 10 | 11 | 12 | 13 | 14 |
| 15 | 16 | 17 | 18 | 19 | 20 | 21 |
| 22 | 23 | 24 | 25 | 26 | 27 | 28 |
| 29 | 30 | 31 | | | | |

## SEPT

| | | | | | | |
|---|---|---|---|---|---|---|
| 1 | 2 | 3 | 4 | 5 | 6 | 7 |
| 8 | 9 | 10 | 11 | 12 | 13 | 14 |
| 15 | 16 | 17 | 18 | 19 | 20 | 21 |
| 22 | 23 | 24 | 25 | 26 | 27 | 28 |
| 29 | 30 | | | | | |

## OCT

| | | | | | | |
|---|---|---|---|---|---|---|
| 1 | 2 | 3 | 4 | 5 | 6 | 7 |
| 8 | 9 | 10 | 11 | 12 | 13 | 14 |
| 15 | 16 | 17 | 18 | 19 | 20 | 21 |
| 22 | 23 | 24 | 25 | 26 | 27 | 28 |
| 29 | 30 | 31 | | | | |

## NOV

| | | | | | | |
|---|---|---|---|---|---|---|
| 1 | 2 | 3 | 4 | 5 | 6 | 7 |
| 8 | 9 | 10 | 11 | 12 | 13 | 14 |
| 15 | 16 | 17 | 18 | 19 | 20 | 21 |
| 22 | 23 | 24 | 25 | 26 | 27 | 28 |
| 29 | 30 | | | | | |

## DEC

| | | | | | | |
|---|---|---|---|---|---|---|
| 1 | 2 | 3 | 4 | 5 | 6 | 7 |
| 8 | 9 | 10 | 11 | 12 | 13 | 14 |
| 15 | 16 | 17 | 18 | 19 | 20 | 21 |
| 22 | 23 | 24 | 25 | 26 | 27 | 28 |
| 29 | 30 | 31 | | | | |

# CALENDAR YEAR 3

## JAN

| | | | | | | |
|---|---|---|---|---|---|---|
| 1 | 2 | 3 | 4 | 5 | 6 | 7 |
| 8 | 9 | 10 | 11 | 12 | 13 | 14 |
| 15 | 16 | 17 | 18 | 19 | 20 | 21 |
| 22 | 23 | 24 | 25 | 26 | 27 | 28 |
| 29 | 30 | 31 | | | | |

## FEB

| | | | | | | |
|---|---|---|---|---|---|---|
| 1 | 2 | 3 | 4 | 5 | 6 | 7 |
| 8 | 9 | 10 | 11 | 12 | 13 | 14 |
| 15 | 16 | 17 | 18 | 19 | 20 | 21 |
| 22 | 23 | 24 | 25 | 26 | 27 | 28 |
| 29 | | | | | | |

## MAR

| | | | | | | |
|---|---|---|---|---|---|---|
| 1 | 2 | 3 | 4 | 5 | 6 | 7 |
| 8 | 9 | 10 | 11 | 12 | 13 | 14 |
| 15 | 16 | 17 | 18 | 19 | 20 | 21 |
| 22 | 23 | 24 | 25 | 26 | 27 | 28 |
| 29 | 30 | 31 | | | | |

## APR

| | | | | | | |
|---|---|---|---|---|---|---|
| 1 | 2 | 3 | 4 | 5 | 6 | 7 |
| 8 | 9 | 10 | 11 | 12 | 13 | 14 |
| 15 | 16 | 17 | 18 | 19 | 20 | 21 |
| 22 | 23 | 24 | 25 | 26 | 27 | 28 |
| 29 | 30 | | | | | |

## MAY

| | | | | | | |
|---|---|---|---|---|---|---|
| 1 | 2 | 3 | 4 | 5 | 6 | 7 |
| 8 | 9 | 10 | 11 | 12 | 13 | 14 |
| 15 | 16 | 17 | 18 | 19 | 20 | 21 |
| 22 | 23 | 24 | 25 | 26 | 27 | 28 |
| 29 | 30 | 31 | | | | |

## JUN

| | | | | | | |
|---|---|---|---|---|---|---|
| 1 | 2 | 3 | 4 | 5 | 6 | 7 |
| 8 | 9 | 10 | 11 | 12 | 13 | 14 |
| 15 | 16 | 17 | 18 | 19 | 20 | 21 |
| 22 | 23 | 24 | 25 | 26 | 27 | 28 |
| 29 | 30 | | | | | |

## JUL

| | | | | | | |
|---|---|---|---|---|---|---|
| 1 | 2 | 3 | 4 | 5 | 6 | 7 |
| 8 | 9 | 10 | 11 | 12 | 13 | 14 |
| 15 | 16 | 17 | 18 | 19 | 20 | 21 |
| 22 | 23 | 24 | 25 | 26 | 27 | 28 |
| 29 | 30 | 31 | | | | |

. . . . . . . . . . . . . . . . . . . . . . . . . . . .
. . . . . . . . . . . . . . . . . . . . . . . . . . . .
. . . . . . . . . . . . . . . . . . . . . . . . . . . .

## AUG

| | | | | | | |
|---|---|---|---|---|---|---|
| 1 | 2 | 3 | 4 | 5 | 6 | 7 |
| 8 | 9 | 10 | 11 | 12 | 13 | 14 |
| 15 | 16 | 17 | 18 | 19 | 20 | 21 |
| 22 | 23 | 24 | 25 | 26 | 27 | 28 |
| 29 | 30 | 31 | | | | |

. . . . . . . . . . . . . . . . . . . . . . . . . . . .
. . . . . . . . . . . . . . . . . . . . . . . . . . . .
. . . . . . . . . . . . . . . . . . . . . . . . . . . .

## SEPT

| | | | | | | |
|---|---|---|---|---|---|---|
| 1 | 2 | 3 | 4 | 5 | 6 | 7 |
| 8 | 9 | 10 | 11 | 12 | 13 | 14 |
| 15 | 16 | 17 | 18 | 19 | 20 | 21 |
| 22 | 23 | 24 | 25 | 26 | 27 | 28 |
| 29 | 30 | | | | | |

. . . . . . . . . . . . . . . . . . . . . . . . . . . .
. . . . . . . . . . . . . . . . . . . . . . . . . . . .
. . . . . . . . . . . . . . . . . . . . . . . . . . . .

## OCT

| | | | | | | |
|---|---|---|---|---|---|---|
| 1 | 2 | 3 | 4 | 5 | 6 | 7 |
| 8 | 9 | 10 | 11 | 12 | 13 | 14 |
| 15 | 16 | 17 | 18 | 19 | 20 | 21 |
| 22 | 23 | 24 | 25 | 26 | 27 | 28 |
| 29 | 30 | 31 | | | | |

. . . . . . . . . . . . . . . . . . . . . . . . . . . .
. . . . . . . . . . . . . . . . . . . . . . . . . . . .
. . . . . . . . . . . . . . . . . . . . . . . . . . . .

## NOV

| | | | | | | |
|---|---|---|---|---|---|---|
| 1 | 2 | 3 | 4 | 5 | 6 | 7 |
| 8 | 9 | 10 | 11 | 12 | 13 | 14 |
| 15 | 16 | 17 | 18 | 19 | 20 | 21 |
| 22 | 23 | 24 | 25 | 26 | 27 | 28 |
| 29 | 30 | | | | | |

. . . . . . . . . . . . . . . . . . . . . . . . . . . .
. . . . . . . . . . . . . . . . . . . . . . . . . . . .
. . . . . . . . . . . . . . . . . . . . . . . . . . . .

## DEC

| | | | | | | |
|---|---|---|---|---|---|---|
| 1 | 2 | 3 | 4 | 5 | 6 | 7 |
| 8 | 9 | 10 | 11 | 12 | 13 | 14 |
| 15 | 16 | 17 | 18 | 19 | 20 | 21 |
| 22 | 23 | 24 | 25 | 26 | 27 | 28 |
| 29 | 30 | 31 | | | | |

. . . . . . . . . . . . . . . . . . . . . . . . . . . .
. . . . . . . . . . . . . . . . . . . . . . . . . . . .
. . . . . . . . . . . . . . . . . . . . . . . . . . . .

# GENERAL SCRIBBLES

# GENERAL SCRIBBLES

# PHOTOS

Stuff an envelope full of photos and memories to decorate your room.

PLACE
ENVELOPE
HERE

PLACE
ENVELOPE
HERE

CPSIA information can be obtained
at www.ICGtesting.com
Printed in the USA
LVOW05*1434180517

535008LV00023B/338/P